D1145000

Globalisation

IRIS TEICHMANN

WANDSWORTH PUBLIC LIBRARY

W
FRANKLIN WATTS
LONDON • SYDNEY

First published in 2002 by Franklin Watts
96 Leonard Street, London EC2A 4XD

Franklin Watts Australia
56 O'Riordan Street
Alexandria, NSW 2015

Copyright © Franklin Watts 2002
Series editor: Rachel Cooke
Series Design: White Design
Picture research: Diana Morris

A CIP catalogue record for this book is available from the British Library.

500765922

ISBN: 0 7496 4440 0

Dewey Classification 337

Printed in Belgium

Acknowledgements:
Toby Adamson/Still Pictures: 17. Shane Batham/Environmental Images: 27t.
Martin Bond/Environmental Images: 14t, 24t, 26. E. Duigenan-Christian Aid/Still Pictures: 13.
Mark Edwards/Still Pictures: 12t, 20b. Julio Etchart/Still Pictures: cover, 8b, 28.
Matthew Fearn/PA Photos: 23t. Ron Giling/Still Pictures: 5b, 6, 12b, 20t.
Paul Glendell/Still Pictures: 29b. David Hoffman/Still Pictures: 16.
Steve Morgan/Environmental Images: 19b. Shehzad Noorani/Still Pictures: 18, 21.
PA Photos/EPA: 5t, 22-23b. Trevor Perry/Environmental Images: 27c.
Latha Raman/Ecoscene: 8t. Thomas Raupach/Still Pictures: 14c.
Eric Schaffer/Ecoscene: 7t. Hartmut Schwarzbach/Still Pictures: 4, 9b, 10, 11b, 15.
Jorgen Schytte/Still Pictures: 11t, 19t. Pankaj Sekhsaria/Environmental Images: 25t.
Rod Smith/Ecoscene: 29t.

Whilst every attempt has been made to clear copyright should there be any inadvertent
omission please apply in the first instance to the publisher regarding rectification.

CONTENTS

WHAT IS GLOBALISATION?

GLOBALISATION *is about us living in a global community. As a result of technological advances in communications – from the telephone to the world wide web – countries are increasingly connected to each other politically, economically, culturally and environmentally.*

A FOCUS OF DEBATE

Many people are concerned about globalisation – in particular the effects of international trade. This is when countries buy and sell goods and services from and to other countries. With the money countries make from exporting goods, they can expand their industries and wealth and improve the standard of living of their own people. At the same time, countries can also use the money they make from exports to import goods and services that they need.

GLOBAL TRADE

After the Second World War, governments saw global trade as a key factor in helping countries recover from the economic ruin of the war. They set up institutions to encourage international trade and slowly new wealth was generated, particularly in the West. But modern trade became truly global in the 1980s. Advances in air travel and communications made transport costs very cheap. Companies could now start to move business and production processes to other countries to save costs.

⬅ *Today, millions of dollars are moved around the world every day. Brokers at stock exchanges, like this one in New York, invest clients' money in companies they think will do well in the future.*

4

← *A poster promoting* **Harry Potter and the Philosopher's Stone** *in China. Globalisation has led to the increased sharing of popular culture.*

GET THE FACTS STRAIGHT

Here are some useful definitions:

- **Goods:** things to sell such as tools, machinery, food items and clothes.
- **Services:** skills such as those provided by electricians, doctors, nurses, teachers, scientists or accountants.
- **To export:** sell goods or services to a buyer outside your own country.
- **To import:** buy and bring into a country goods or services from another country.
- **An economy:** the organisation of a nation's money and resources, especially in relation to goods and services.

THE MOVE TO FREE TRADE

One of the driving factors behind the move to global trade is countries trading as if there are no national borders. A few decades ago, most countries imposed fees, or tariffs, on imported goods making them expensive – and less of a threat to locally-produced goods. But today every country is encouraged to drop these tariffs. This is known as free trade. Global free trade allows countries to specialise, improving products and services. As a result we can now choose products from all over the world, sold at lower prices than in the past.

→ *Workers in a factory in India producing shoes for a Western shoe company. The company has moved its production to India to benefit from cheaper labour costs.*

AFTER THE SECOND World War, world leaders saw that the best way to ensure future security and prosperity was to create economic stability through free trade. To this end, governments around the world agreed to set up three important inter-governmental financial institutions – nicknamed the financial trio. This trio not only help manage world trade and finance, but have a profound effect on the process of globalisation.

THE WORLD BANK

The World Bank was originally set up to help rebuild war-damaged economies in Europe. Now, it uses money from its 183 member countries to provide loans to those member countries that need help to develop their economies and take part in free global trade. The poorest member countries can get interest-free loans from the World Bank for up to 50 years. Better-off countries can also get loans to help them improve their economy, but they have to pay some interest on their loans.

⬇ Workers help construct the Hahaile Dam in Ethiopia with money from the World Bank. They get six kilos of grain in return for six hours of work.

THE IMF

The International Monetary Fund (IMF) was set up at the same time as the World Bank. It also gets its money from its 183 member countries. It watches the rates at which money is exchanged around the world, aiming to keep these rates stable. It also gives loans to member countries if they have run into debt they cannot pay back. In return, they have to allow foreign investment in their country and the free flow of capital, goods and services across their borders.

⬆ Goods transported by ship are unloaded at a port. Import tariffs may well be charged on some of them.

GET THE FACTS STRAIGHT

The main international agreements are:

● General Agreement on Tariffs and Trade (GATT): in 1947, member countries agreed to freely trade in goods such as food, minerals and manufactured goods.

● General Agreement on Trade in Services (GATS): member countries agreed in 1994 to freely trade in services, such as banking, telecommunications, education and healthcare.

● Trade-Related Aspects of Intellectual Property Rights (TRIPS): in 1994, it was agreed that when a company creates something artistic (a book, a piece of music etc), invents something or develops something new in the field of science or industry, no one else can copy it without permission from that company. Intellectual Property Rights can be referred to as copyright or patents.

GATT WHAT?

From 1947 until 1995, the General Agreement on Tariffs and Trade (GATT) promoted free trade among countries around the world and reduced the many barriers that countries had imposed on each other. The last negotiations took place in Uruguay during 1986 to 1994, as a result of which governments agreed to allow a better flow of services, such as banking and travel, into their countries. In 1995, GATT was replaced with the World Trade Organisation (WTO).

WTO WHO?

The WTO has 139 member countries, who negotiate trade agreements amongst themselves. If two countries have a dispute over trade, the WTO can help resolve the issue. It also has the power to allow member countries to ban or restrict imports from other countries if these break existing international laws and regulations.

GLOBALISATION hit the news around the world in November 1999 when violent clashes between anti-globalisation protesters and the police severely disrupted the World Trade Organisation meeting in Seattle, USA. Over 40,000 people, including representatives from 700 organisations and charities, were there to raise some serious issues about globalisation. Similar protests have occurred at WTO meetings ever since.

⬇ *Protesters march against globalisation. These voices have become louder and more persistent across the developed world.*

↗ *The commercial centre of Mumbai, India overlooks vast slums, highlighting the gap between rich and poor.*

WORLD POVERTY

Most agree that trade is essential for any country to develop economically. Yet some 1.3 billion people in the world still live in absolute poverty. The poorest countries in the world do not even have the infrastructure (transport and communications) to produce goods. Even the World Bank admits that the poorest countries, mainly in Africa, have actually got poorer over the last few decades despite the increase in free world trade. These countries, the anti-globalisation groups say, simply cannot compete in a world of free trade.

CORPORATE CONTROL

Many people today object to the way that governments bend over backwards to accommodate the demands of big companies in order to make sure they invest in their country. Some governments have even gone so far as to make less money available for public services so that big companies can pay less tax.

This situation is further complicated by human rights issues. For example, China has developed its economy by allowing foreign companies to pay less tax when they invest in China. Yet many people argue that companies investing in China are indirectly supporting the government there, and so are tolerating its human rights abuses. Others say, by contrast, that it opens China up to foreign influence which will eventually lead to political change.

CONSUMERISM

Global trade and international co-operation have brought many benefits, especially to Western countries. We live much longer, can cure many more diseases and lead comfortable lives. Yet some people are questioning the value of having too much to choose from and whether the ambition to earn more and more money is a healthy one. Some people go further and say that Western consumerism, such as the WTO promotes, should not be a role model for developing countries.

➡️ *Is it right that we can choose from such a huge range of products at the supermarket?*

WHAT DO YOU THINK?

The WTO has become a particular focus of anti-globalisation protests because it promotes free trade above all else. This campaigner imagines how the WTO could affect positive action for the environment: "Imagine your government passes a law, which prohibits any action that in any way damages the environment. Imagine further that another country decides to challenge this because under the free trade rules it should be allowed to sell a product that could potentially have harmful effects on the environment. The WTO's role is to promote free trade and it will therefore normally rule in favour of the country that wants to export the goods."

How do you think someone in favour of globalisation might reply to this?

WE ARE ALL FAMILIAR with top brand names such as Coca-Cola, Nike or Microsoft. But can you name the ten biggest international companies off the top of your head? The majority of the top ten global corporations deal with less glamorous products such as pesticides, veterinary medicine, pharmaceuticals and commercial seeds. Yet these companies dominate two-thirds of world trade. Not surprisingly, many smaller companies find it hard to compete.

⬆ *People in developing countries like China or India often prefer Western products to products made in their own country because of the familiarity of the product name.*

MONEY, MONEY, MONEY

Companies are always looking to find new markets to increase their profits. If a company has established a brand name at home, it may buy up other companies and look to expand its trade abroad. To cut costs, it may move its production to countries with cheaper labour, as free trade laws promote. In this way it makes more profit. It also creates work for local people in the country it invests in, who gradually earn more and therefore spend more. This helps boost the domestic economy. Developing countries like China and Mexico, for example, have been able to successfully build up their economies in this way.

LOCAL IMPACT

However, multi-national companies can also seriously threaten the livelihood of local producers and their industries. Indian car companies have no chance of surviving on the world market against some of the major car companies of developed countries. Some developing countries have tried to market their own soft drinks, but cannot compete with the American multi-national soft drinks companies like Coca-Cola or Pepsi.

⬆ *Poor communication and roads, like this one in Eritrea in Africa, deter investment from Western companies.*

JOBS FOR EVERYONE?

Some people say that multi-national companies increase economic growth and create jobs. Others say that the power of these companies creates job insecurity as a company can easily move its factories elsewhere if labour costs become too high. They also point out that the least developed countries cannot benefit – places like Ethiopia or Somalia do not have the infrastructure to attract such investment.

GET THE FACTS STRAIGHT

- Between 1980 and 1995, the top 100 global companies made 679% more profit. But they also employed 8% fewer people.

- Global corporations buy up other companies. This is called a merger. This way, they get bigger and make it impossible for smaller companies to compete. They may effectively have sole control of a particular market. Trillions of dollars are spent every year on mergers.

- Three companies deal with 83% of world trade in cocoa, six companies control 85% of world trade in grain and three companies deal with 80% of world trade in bananas.

➡ *Unemployed people wait to claim their welfare payments in Germany. If Western companies move factories abroad, they take job opportunities away from local people.*

GLOBAL DEBT

MOST COUNTRIES HAVE DEBTS *for many reasons: they import more than they export, they do not make enough money from the goods they do export or they need money to build up their infrastructure. Many poorer countries use a lot of money to fight wars. Sometimes debts can become too great to manage.*

BORROWED WORLD

Less developed countries are particularly affected by debt. Countries like Brazil, Kenya, Guatemala and Nicaragua produce lots of coffee. Over the years, coffee prices have gone down. This means that coffee-producing countries cannot make enough money to pay for the food and goods that they need to import. They borrow money from other countries and from the World Bank or the IMF.

← A poster in Ghana encourages people to export more to earn the country much-needed cash.

⬆ A family living in a slum in Argentina, a country deeply in debt.

THE PRICE OF OIL

But there are other factors that contribute to debt. Oil-producing countries control the price of oil by changing how much oil they produce. In the 1970s, demand for oil was high and oil prices went up. This affected all countries, but less developed countries, in particular, had to borrow money to pay for their fuel bills. The higher oil prices also increased the cost of producing goods, resulting in less profit when they exported them. With less income, and interest to pay on the debt, they became more in debt.

HELP AT HAND?

The World Bank lends money to countries in this position so that they can pay off their debts and build up their infrastructure to attract foreign investment. In turn, these countries have to open up their markets to imports that then compete with their own domestic products. At the same time, they have to push their own exports into the world market to earn enough money to pay their debts. However, it can be difficult for these exports to compete successfully with established brands from the developed world.

DROP DEBT?

Many argue that countries owing money to the World Bank should not have to pay back their debts. Otherwise they will be unable to fight poverty and develop their economy. Some 150 developing countries have borrowed money, and some do manage to pay off their debts. However, many get into difficulty by wasting the money they have been lent through corruption, fighting wars or simply through mismanagement.

GET THE FACTS STRAIGHT

This is a simple example of how debt can grow. Imagine the far greater sums involved in loans to developing countries:

- The bank agrees to lend £500 at 10% interest a month.
- At the end of the month, the debtor pays the interest only, that is £50, so the loan does not decrease nor the interest.
- The next month, the debtor manages to pay only £30, so the debt increases to £520 and the interest now owed next month to £52.
- The next month, the debtor pays £45 so the debt is now £527 and the interest £52.70. Slowly the debt burden grows.

A group of Westerners campaign for governments to drop global debt.

A derelict farm surrounded by vast wheatfields in the UK. Many small farms have been unable to compete in the global market.

Red peppers are harvested in the Netherlands, a market leader in the mass production of fruit and vegetables.

DO YOU EVER think about where the food you eat actually comes from? For most of us, food simply comes from the supermarket. We tend to choose the food that we like, and often choose the cheapest on offer.

MONOCULTURES

Supermarkets tend to buy much of their food from large, industrial farms that concentrate on growing one type of food. These are called monocultures. The Netherlands, for example, has huge farms growing tomatoes and cucumbers for export into other European countries. These are much cheaper than locally-grown tomatoes or cucumbers.

CASH CROPS

The international push towards free trade has led to many small-scale farmers in Asia and Africa, who traditionally produced food for their own consumption, growing cash crops. This means they grow food to sell rather than consume. In a bid to make more profit, they may switch to growing crops that might not be suitable for the land, or adopt Western farming practices that may lead to environmental damage.

FACING THE ISSUES

In 1995 the Mozambique government decided to build up its local industry of processing raw cashew nuts. They introduced a system whereby processed cashew nuts could be exported freely but raw cashew nuts could only be exported if the farmer paid an export tax to the government.

Mozambique owes debts to the World Bank. The Bank told the Mozambique government to remove the export tax as a condition of its loan and said that it would make more money by exporting raw cashew nuts. It now seems this was not the right decision; since then, the price of nuts has fallen. Mozambique missed the opportunity to build up a new industry which would have created jobs. By becoming a specialist in the processing of raw cashew nuts, the country could also have offered something extra to the world market, enabling it to compete more effectively.

VICIOUS CIRCLE

Farmers of cash crops effectively produce less food for themselves. The result is that their country eventually needs to import much needed food items, sometimes at a price they cannot afford. Meanwhile, their farmers have to compete with food imports from other countries. If the country's main economy is based on agriculture, it may eventually run into debt and have to pay interest on loans from the World Bank. If it cannot improve its economic position, it will spiral even further into debt.

MORE CONTROL?

Too much food on the global market means cheaper food but lower incomes for farmers worldwide. Western farmers – affected by cheap imports as much as farmers in less developed countries – get financial help from their governments to survive. But millions of farmers elsewhere not only get less income from their crops, but are forced out of the global food market altogether. They are forced straight into poverty and even starvation.

A worker on a Kenyan coffee farm. Kenyan coffee is exported all over the world.

MAYBE YOU HAVE already heard about fair-trade products? In the West, demand for fair-trade goods is gradually growing but fair-trade companies still have to convince the public at large that fair trade is not just charity but a modern business concept that benefits all.

⬇ *This Venezuelan cocoa farm has over 3,000 cocoa trees – it is big enough to produce cocoa beans for export.*

FAIR PRICE

Most cocoa producers sell their products to intermediaries who buy at the lowest possible price. They sell the goods on to an international company. The company then exports the cocoa into other countries. With so many people trying to make a profit, this leaves most cocoa farmers with hardly enough money to survive. Fair trade aims to help these farmers. If you choose to buy a fair-traded chocolate bar, for example, you will pay slightly more than you would for other brands of chocolate. The extra money you pay then goes directly back to the local producers in cocoa-producing countries.

A DECENT LIVELIHOOD

The higher price paid for fair-traded goods means that local farmers can make a proper living and do not have to migrate to cities. But fair trade is not just about survival. It allows communities to support local clinics or schools, or buy new technology to develop their trade. With more money in their pockets, people can choose to buy local food rather than cheaper imported food. Fair trade also encourages sustainable, non-polluting farming practices.

GET THE FACTS STRAIGHT

Fair-trade companies operate along the following principles:

● They trade directly with the local producers. The money fair-trade companies save that way goes directly to the producers.

● They ensure the producers have good working conditions, are aware of environmental issues and that no one is exploited.

● They often provide advice, training and support to help develop the products.

● They will usually only deal with producers in Africa, Asia and Latin America who, on their own, are unable to sell their goods on the world market, or with companies that have good social and environmental policies.

A FAIR FUTURE?

Western consumers are not always aware of how fair trade works and often think that buying fair-trade products is like giving money to charities – not sure where the money actually ends up and whether it really benefits the people it is supposed to. This may well be because there is not yet a very wide range of fair-trade products available in our mainstream supermarkets. It may also be that fair-trade companies need to do more about communicating the message to consumers that buying a fair-trade product actually makes a huge difference to local producers. At the end of the day, for fair trade to work, it depends on each of us to make the connection between what we buy and where it came from.

→ Chocolate is one of the most popular fair-trade products available in shops in the West.

RIGHTS TO THE BASICS

SUPPORTERS *of global free trade say that opening up global markets helps less developed countries to earn enough to improve their health and education systems. But anti-globalisation campaigners argue that the opposite is actually the case. No one would disagree that the problems below exist, but those in favour of globalisation would claim a country must be part of the global economy in order to resolve them. Those against would call for alternative solutions.*

PRIVATISATION

As many less developed countries have switched from growing local food to growing food for export, they have lost money as world food prices have come down. The loans they receive from the World Bank come with conditions. It means that governments of these countries are forced to spend less money on important public services like health care or water supplies. As a result, these public services are then run by private companies who often charge high prices for essential services.

➡ *A girl in Bangladesh attends school at the same time as looking after the younger members of her family.*

FACING THE ISSUES

Ghanaian farmers used to grow enough rice to feed the people of Ghana. This changed when the World Bank gave Ghana a loan to concentrate on gold and cocoa exports and improve its economy. Many rice farmers moved to the cities to work in these developing industries. Ghana had to begin importing rice for people to eat, at a high price. Unfortunately, the increased money made from gold and cocoa exports did not cover the new cost of food imports. So, the Ghanaian government had to cut the money it spent on public services, in order to pay back the loan and the interest on the loan. The Ghanaian people now have to pay for clean water or seeing a doctor, when they can barely afford to buy enough food.

↑ In rural Ghana, people rely on one water pump in their village for their daily water.

↓ HIV and AIDS education in South Africa. The country won a battle to produce a cheap version of a patented medicine to treat HIV.

WATER FOR ALL

We don't think twice about paying our water companies to provide us with clean, safe drinking water. But in less developed countries, where industries and households in the cities have ever higher demands for water, they compete with poorer people outside the cities who need the water to survive and to grow food. Water is also an issue for the Western world. Tourism has put a considerable strain on water resources in hot spots like the Grand Canyon in the US and the Mediterranean coastal resorts.

DOES WEALTH MEAN HEALTH?

Modern science has not yet found a way to create water out of nothing. But it has developed medicines to increase our life expectancy dramatically – yet these medicines do not come cheaply. Many Western pharmaceutical companies have their drugs patented, using the TRIPS agreement (see page 7). This means no one else except the company itself can make the drug. Yet millions of people in less developed countries cannot afford to pay for the drugs at Western prices.

RICHER OR POORER?

DOES GLOBALISATION *actually make us richer? The income gap between the world's poorest and the world's richest countries has in fact widened since the 1960s. Research also shows that the average American worker earns 10 per cent less today than ten years ago – taking into account inflation. Global trade means that Western workers do not just compete amongst themselves but also with workers from less developed countries.*

⬆ *Mass production in an Indian factory. The pressure to keep costs down can lead to workers' rights being abused.*

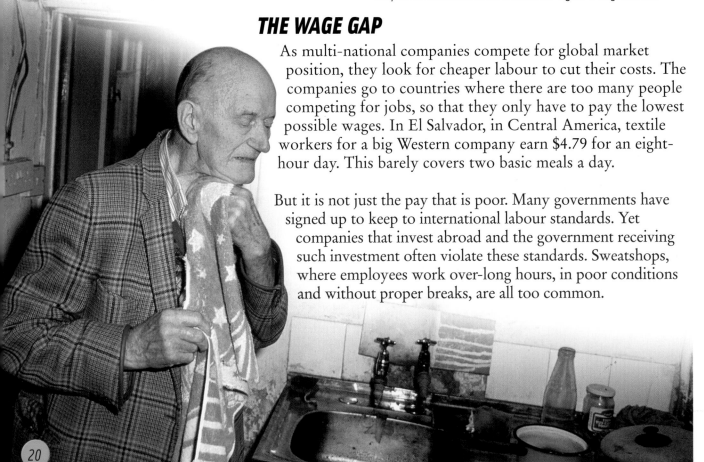

⬇ *This old man lives in terrible poverty despite coming from the developed Western world.*

THE WAGE GAP

As multi-national companies compete for global market position, they look for cheaper labour to cut their costs. The companies go to countries where there are too many people competing for jobs, so that they only have to pay the lowest possible wages. In El Salvador, in Central America, textile workers for a big Western company earn $4.79 for an eight-hour day. This barely covers two basic meals a day.

But it is not just the pay that is poor. Many governments have signed up to keep to international labour standards. Yet companies that invest abroad and the government receiving such investment often violate these standards. Sweatshops, where employees work over-long hours, in poor conditions and without proper breaks, are all too common.

BONDED LABOUR

Slavery – the ownership of a human being – was abolished in the 19th century. Yet in the 21st century, there are still millions of people around the world who live in slave-like conditions. There are some 20 million people who are held in bonded labour. This happens when a worker 'sells' himself to an employer in order to borrow money, hoping to pay the debt off through work over time. Yet it becomes impossible to pay off the debt because the 'employer' charges money for food and accommodation or increases the interest rate on the loan. The worker cannot leave because of the debt and is thus trapped.

WHAT DO YOU THINK?

- Would you knowingly buy a product that had been produced by people working in poor conditions?
- How can you be certain that a product has not been produced in this way?
- What can you do to find out more about the way the goods you buy are produced?

GLOBAL HOPE

While globalisation has in some cases contributed to poorer working conditions, it has also helped to push governments together to set up international laws to tackle them. Both the United Nations and the European Union have set up initiatives on bonded labour. The public is also becoming increasingly aware of its power as a consumer. Charities run campaigns to highlight the plight of workers, naming individual companies who use this type of labour. Corrupt governments or companies who turn a blind eye to forced and bonded labour, or are even involved in it, find it more and more difficult to escape international scrutiny. Globalisation is here to stay but with tighter controls perhaps it could help improve lives everywhere, rather than in selected areas.

⬇ *This Bangladeshi boy works in a tanners where leather is made. We may find it shocking, but he probably has to work to help his family survive.*

ETHICAL INVESTMENT

WHAT DO YOU DO with your pocket money? If you put it into your savings account, you know that you will earn interest on your money. The way that banks make the money to be able to pay you interest is by lending money to others. Banks charge fees and interest on the money they lend to big companies, and so make a good profit. But how would you feel if you knew that your bank was lending your money to cosmetic companies who regularly test their products on animals?

IMMORAL MONEY

Many major high street banks have for years lent money to companies who have been involved in damaging the environment. Banks can, knowingly or unknowingly, also end up lending money to companies that use child or forced labour. Or they may help companies who want to set up business in countries with poor human-rights records. Some financial companies have recently decided not to do business in Burma because of the military regime there that abuses human rights.

WHAT DO YOU THINK?

- Are there any issues that you feel strongly about?
- How can you find out whether your bank lends money to companies who engage in activities you strongly disagree with?
- Would you or your parents consider switching banks?
- How would you choose an alternative bank?
- What criteria will the new bank have to fulfil before you are willing to invest your money with them?

COUNTRIES IN ARMS

Lending money to companies who sell arms to countries where these weapons are used to kill people is considered to be one of the most unethical practices that banks can adopt. Most of us do not know whether our banks lend money to such companies when we trust them with our money. Yet it is likely that most of the high street banks in your area do. Some people don't mind. They argue that lending money to arms companies can help create jobs and develop technology.

⬆ Most people in the developed world today keep their money in a bank and enjoy the convenience of cash machines. But do they know how the bank is investing their money?

⬅ These United Nations soldiers are dependent on weapons to protect civilians in Sierra Leone from rebel activities. Some people suggest that the arms trade encourages local disputes, such as that in Sierra Leone, to become violent and out of control.

TO ARM OR NOT TO ARM?

More and more people disagree with supporting arms companies in any way. They say that selling arms is actually a silent agreement that they will be used to kill a person somewhere else in the world. For some, this view is too simplistic. They point out that many people in the world still have to fight for democracy in their country. They also argue that countries not only need arms to enforce peace around the world, but also to be able to defend themselves.

CLIMATE CHANGE

TODAY, MANY COUNTRIES *experience more extreme weather conditions than ever before. In 1998, Hurricane Mitch devastated Honduras and Nicaragua, countries already struggling to pay back their million-dollar foreign debts. Europe has seen terrible flooding in recent years; Australia's coral reef is losing its colour and dying because of the rising sea temperature, and there are many more examples worldwide.*

⬆ *Cars have become so affordable that many households have two. Increased traffic means that in cities traffic can be as slow as it was a hundred years ago.*

BUSY TRADING

The huge increase in global trade means that far more goods are transported around the world by plane, lorry, ship and train. Large industrial farms replace human and animal energy with energy burnt from fossil fuels. We produce more pesticides and packaged products. Free trade encourages less developed countries to catch up with buying energy-using goods. In China, this means that its huge, over one billion population will increasingly turn to cars, and not bicycles, as their preferred mode of transport.

Pollution rises from a steel works in India. As developing countries become more industrialised, they too contribute to environmental pollution.

WHO IS TO BLAME?

Most people agree that the change in the weather is due to global warming. Some natural factors contribute to global warming. Some scientists say that global warming is due to the sun getting periodically hotter. But most experts agree that the unnatural increase in greenhouse gases over the last 50 years is down to increased energy consumption. Yet, while world governments generally agree that climate change is happening, not all recognise that there is a link between global warming and economic globalisation.

WHAT DO YOU THINK?

Even though most governments have accepted the reality of global warming, experts warn that we need to change our way of life faster than we think.

● How do you get around each day? Where do you shop? What links can you see between this and global trade? How does it connect with global warming?

● Do you know of any alternative ways of producing energy in your country?

● Some people say less developed countries should be told to look after the environment first before becoming consumer societies like Western countries. Do you think this is right?

● Can you have free global trade but also have strict environmental standards that companies have to comply with before they can trade?

WHAT CAN GOVERNMENTS DO?

Some governments have taken measures against environmental damage, such as imposing fines on companies who pollute the environment, or restricting traffic into inner city areas. But many fear that as developing countries engage more and more in trade and production, they will add an additional burden to world pollution.

THE KYOTO PROTOCOL

Much pollution is caused by gases emitted from industry. In 1992, governments of developed countries agreed not to increase these gas emissions. Then in 1999, they actually agreed, in the Kyoto Protocol, to reduce their emissions. However, few have kept to the agreement. This table shows the percentage increase of emissions in developed countries since then.

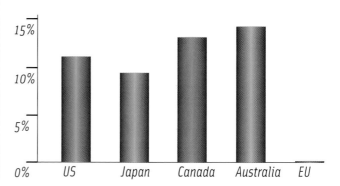

Source: The Ecologist

WHAT THINGS DO YOU do every day that consume energy? Any of these: eating imported food, using the car rather than walking to school, coming home with shopping bags full of packaged products or playing games on your computer? And what have you thrown away today? The more we consume, the more we throw away.

WASTED EFFORTS?

The United Nations' Environmental Programme estimates that since 1980, people in Western Europe alone have increased their waste production by 35 per cent. Waste costs money and energy. All this waste needs to be transported to landfill sites, which are now filling up and also causing environmental hazards. Some cities opt for the use of incinerators to burn the waste. This, they argue, helps produce energy, although local residents often worry about health risks posed by the gases that are emitted during the burning process. Successful recycling schemes are in place in many Western countries, but most do not recycle plastic because the initial start-up costs to do so are huge.

GET THE FACTS STRAIGHT

Here are some environmental success stories:

- Iceland aims to stop using fossil fuels completely by 2030 and to use hydrogen fuel-cell technology instead.
- The Lombardy region in Italy aims to ban totally the sale of new petrol- and diesel-powered cars to reduce the serious air pollution which damages people's health and the area's historic buildings.
- European countries like France, Germany and Italy organise regular car-free Sundays, where only public transport is allowed.
- Denmark and the United Kingdom are planning to develop the use of wind power to produce up to a third of their countries' electricity over the next few decades.
- In the Netherlands, bicycle ownership is much higher than car ownership and many cycle to work every day.

Mass consumerism produces mass waste. Yet all the products shown here could be recycled if facilities were available.

⬈ The Great Barrier Reef in Australia is threatened by both oil exploration and climate change.

➡ Few people have considered the effects on the environment resulting from the huge increase in air travel.

DYING WILDLIFE

Wildlife around the world faces other dangers because we consume more energy. You may have seen pictures of oil-covered birds after one of the recent oil tanker disasters. The quest for oil in particular can cause environmental disasters. The Australian government may allow a US oil company to drill for oil in the Great Barrier Reef area. This not only threatens the various whale, turtle and dolphin species, but could also harm the reef itself, which is already suffering from an increase in the ocean temperature due to global warming.

TAKE A DEEP BREATH

At any time, there may be up to 10,000 aeroplanes above us, not to mention the billions of cars in cities around the world. While most of us would accept that air pollution is a fact of modern life, not everyone would accept that we should all think before we make a car or plane journey. In cities like London, more and more people are suffering from asthma. Air pollution could be a factor.

UNTIL RECENTLY, *many people thought that it was the government's responsibility to take action against poverty, injustice and environmental pollution. Yet more and more people today are becoming increasingly aware that the choices we make every day can have a direct impact on the lives of individuals thousands of kilometres away. They can also have a direct impact on our local environment, and on the health of our planet as a whole.*

⬇ *Many people nowadays recycle their magazines and newspapers when facilities become available.*

INFORMED CHOICES

Today, we have a wealth of information at our fingertips about the impact companies and their products have on people's lives and our environment (see page 31). There are also many organisations that actively campaign against injustice, poverty and pollution. If we choose to, we can avoid goods that have been produced by children in bonded labour, or food that is sold by companies that exploit farmers financially. By buying fair-trade or environmentally-friendly products, we are both expressing an opinion and contributing to a process of change. It is important to remember that it is consumer choices that drive what industry produces.

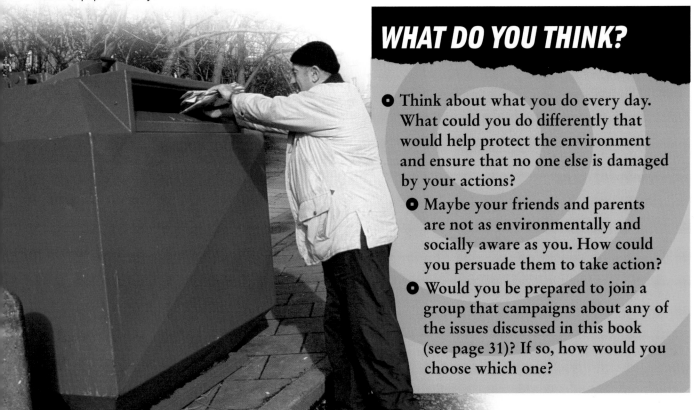

WHAT DO YOU THINK?

- Think about what you do every day. What could you do differently that would help protect the environment and ensure that no one else is damaged by your actions?
  - Maybe your friends and parents are not as environmentally and socially aware as you. How could you persuade them to take action?
  - Would you be prepared to join a group that campaigns about any of the issues discussed in this book (see page 31)? If so, how would you choose which one?

PAY AS YOU POLLUTE

Many companies produce products that are known to be damaging the environment. Car companies do not have to pay for the environmental damage caused by the increased production and use of cars. Many argue for a change of attitude so that companies would pay an environment tax to help offset the damage caused by pollution.

INDIVIDUAL RESPONSIBILITY

But it is not just companies who need to take responsibility. If we decide to recycle our household waste, get on our bicycles, use less water and energy, buy recycled material and local foods, we can make a difference. Some governments are changing and are promoting public transport, restricting car use in cities and promoting the use of power suppliers who invest in alternative energy sources, such as wind and solar power – but it is ultimately pressure from its citizens that causes governments to act.

⊙ *Cycling is a cheap, quick and healthy way of getting about – but cycling on car-filled roads can be dangerous.*

⊙ *Recently more and more farmers' markets have sprung up where people can buy fresh, locally-produced food.*

29

GLOSSARY

bonded labour: Workers bound to their employers by debt.

capital: Money or wealth used to produce goods and services or to generate an income.

cash crops: Crops produced to be sold for profit, not for the farmer's consumption.

consumerism: An economy or lifestyle based on an ever-increasing purchase of goods.

copyright: The sole right to reproduce a piece of art, literature or music.

corporation: A company made up of several smaller groups or companies operating together.

debt: Money owed.

democracy: Government by the people or their elected representitives.

economic growth: Increasing production of goods and services and hence income.

economy: The organisation of a nation's money and resources.

ethical: Relating to morals.

export: Selling goods or services to a buyer outside your own country.

fossil fuels: Carbon-based fuels, such as coal, oil and gas, which produce carbon dioxide gas when burnt.

free trade: Trade where no tariffs are charged.

global warming: The increase in temperature of the Earth's atmosphere partly caused by the build-up of greenhouse gases.

goods: Things to sell such as tools, food or clothes.

greenhouse gases: Gases, such as carbon dioxide, that trap heat inside the Earth's atmosphere, as glass does in a greenhouse.

import: Buying goods or services from another country into your country.

income: Money earned or coming in.

inflation: The increase in price of goods and services over time.

infrastructure: The structure and systems around which a country operates on a day-to-day basis, including things such as roads, airports, banks and hospitals.

intellectual property: Refers to the ownership of a concept or an idea, such as a piece of writing or an invention.

interest: Additional payments made on a loan over and above the actual sum of money lent. Banks also pay interest on the savings people keep in the bank.

investment: Money spent on a company to improve its production of goods or services and so its profitability.

labour: The available work force.

loan: Money borrowed, usually from a bank, on which the borrower has to pay interest.

monoculture: A farm specialising in growing one type of crop.

patent: A document given by a government which grants the holder the exclusive right to profit from an invention.

pharmaceutical: Relating to the production of medicine.

quota: A fixed amount of goods.

services: Skills such as those provided by electricians, doctors, scientists or teachers.

tariff: Taxes charged on imported goods.

tax: A charge made by a government.

trade: The buying and selling of goods and services.

FURTHER INFORMATION

INTER-GOVERNMENTAL ORGANISATIONS

International Monetary Fund (IMF)
www.imf.org

International Labour Organisation
www.ilo.org
An off-shoot of the United Nations concerned with promoting workers' rights.

Organisation for Economic Co-operation and Development
www.oecd.org
A research network bringing together 30 member countries to discuss economic and social issues.

The World Bank
www.worldbank.org

World Trade Organisation (WTO)
www.wto.org

United Nations (UN)
www.un.org

NON-GOVERNMENTAL ORGANISATIONS

Anti-Slavery International
www.antislavery.org
Oldest international human rights organisation set up in 1839 to campaign against slavery. Works to eliminate any modern forms of slavery.

Campaign Against Arms Trade
www.caat.org.uk
A UK-based organisation campaigning for the end of international arms' trade.

Corporate Watch
www.corpwatch.org
Monitors multi-national companies and what social, economic and ecological impact they have.

Friends of the Earth
www.foe.org
Has the largest international environmental network in the world with associated groups in 63 countries to campaign on environmental issues.

International Forum on Globalisation
www.ifg.org
Set up in 1994, this international forum brings together campaigners and researchers to think about global economic issues and raise public awareness.

One World
www.oneworld.net
An internet-based information centre linking over 1000 organisations to promote human rights and sustainable development.

Oxfam
www.oxfam.org
An international organisation with offices around the world which aims to eliminate poverty.

People and Planet
www.peopleandplanet.net
An electronic magazine published by the UK-based organisation Planet 21. Covers a wide range of issues affecting people and our planet.

Third World Network
www.twnside.org.sg
An independent non-profit international network of organisations and individuals involved in development issues.

World Development Movement
www.wdm.org.uk
Set up in 1970, brings together individuals and community groups to lobby for changes in laws and policies in developed countries to help people in less developed countries.

WTO Watch
www.wtowatch.org
Set up by the American Institute for Agriculture and Trade. Has comprehensive information about the WTO, trade and sustainable development issues.

INDEX